I0815541

EVERYTHING SPORTS
EVERYTHING
NHL
BY DONNA McKINNEY
eureka!

Eureka! books turn real stories into unforgettable experiences. This nonfiction imprint sparks curiosity, encourages critical thinking, and engages middle-grade readers. *Eureka!* books empower young minds to explore the stories of the real world, one fascinating fact at a time. Unravel the power of knowledge and lifelong learning with *Eureka!*

This edition first published in 2026 by Bellwether Media, Inc.

Library of Congress Cataloging-in-Publication Data

Names: McKinney, Donna B. (Donna Bowen) author
Title: Everything NHL / By Donna McKinney. Other titles: Everything National Hockey League
Description: Eureka!. | Minneapolis, Minnesota : Bellwether Media, Inc, 2026. | Series: Everything sports | Includes index. | Audience: Ages 9-15 | Audience: Grades 7-9 | Summary: "Engaging images accompany information on NHL. The text level and subject matter are intended for students in grades 5 through 9" -- Provided by publisher.
Identifiers: LCCN 2025021809 (print) | LCCN 2025021810 (ebook) | ISBN 9798893045611 library binding | ISBN 9798893046991 ebook
Subjects: LCSH: National Hockey League--History--Juvenile literature | Stanley Cup (Hockey)--History--Juvenile literature | Hockey--Canada--History--Juvenile literature | Hockey--United States--History--Juvenile literature
Classification: LCC GV847.8.N3 M37 2026 (print) | LCC GV847.8.N3 (ebook) | DDC 796.962/6406--dc23/eng/20250616
LC record available at https://lccn.loc.gov/2025021809
LC ebook record available at https://lccn.loc.gov/2025021810

Editor: Kieran Downs Designer: Jeffrey Kollock

Printed in the United States of America, North Mankato, MN.

TABLE OF CONTENTS

NHL

GOLDEN MISFITS

It is the 2023 Stanley Cup Finals. The Vegas Golden Knights and the Florida Panthers are playing. The Golden Knights are a new team in the National Hockey League (NHL), having played their first game in 2017. Players from other NHL teams were gathered to form the new team. Because of this, the Golden Knights became known as the "Golden Misfits." Despite being a new team, the Golden Knights are already playing in their second-ever Finals.

In Game 5 of the best-of-seven series, the Golden Knights hold a 3–1 series lead. In the first period, the Golden Knights open up the scoring with a goal from Mark Stone. Nicolas Hague adds another goal later in the period to give the Golden Knights an early 2–0 lead. The Panthers answer with a goal of their own in the second period. But the Golden Knights add four more goals before the period is over. They lead 6–1. The Golden Knights score again in the third period. The Panthers answer with two goals of their own. But Mark Stone soon scores his third goal of the night. He completes a **hat trick**! Nicolas Roy adds one more goal for the Golden Knights. The final score is 9–3. The Golden Knights' nine goals tie the NHL record for most goals in one game of a Stanley Cup Final. In just their sixth season, they are Stanley Cup champions!

NICOLAS ROY

STANLEY CUP

The Stanley Cup is named after Lord Stanley of Preston, the former Governor General of Canada. It is the oldest professional sports trophy in North America.

MARK STONE

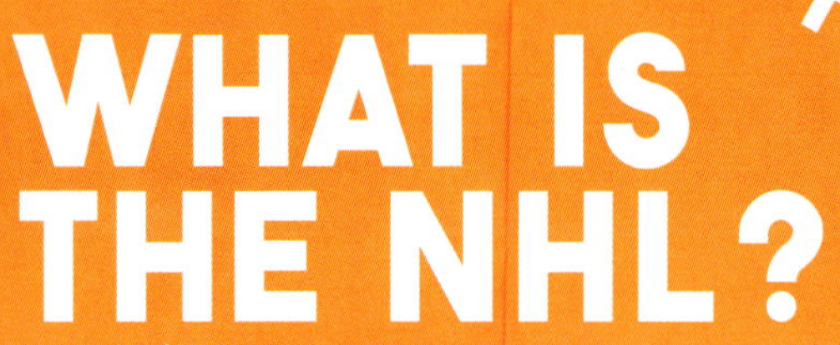

WHAT IS THE NHL?

The NHL is a professional hockey league in North America. There are 32 teams in the NHL. These teams are located in cities in the United States and Canada. The players on these teams come from countries around the world. The 32 teams are divided into the Eastern **Conference** and Western Conference. Within the Eastern Conference, teams are grouped into the Metropolitan **Division** and Atlantic Division. Within the Western Conference, the teams are divided into the Central Division and the Pacific Division.

Many NHL players get their start playing for **minor league** teams. The American Hockey League (AHL) and the East Coast Hockey League (ECHL) are two minor leagues. All of the NHL teams have an **affiliate** team in the AHL. Many NHL teams also have a team in the ECHL.

AHL GAME

SUBSTITUTIONS

Hockey teams can substitute players without a time-out during gameplay.

NHL TEAMS

NHL DRAFT

The NHL **Draft** is the process where NHL teams choose new players. The draft happens each year in June during the league's **offseason**. Teams take turns choosing players who have played in junior hockey leagues, college, or European leagues.

The NHL **preseason** starts in late September and runs for about two weeks. Preseason games do not count toward a team's record. The regular season starts in early October and ends in April.

NHL teams play 82 games in the regular season. Teams play half of their games at their home arenas and play the other games at their opponents' arenas. Teams play three or four games against divisional opponents each season and three games against non-divisional opponents from their conference. They play against teams from the other conference twice per year.

The NHL uses overtime play to decide the winner in tied games. In overtime, teams play for an extra 5 minutes. The first to score wins. If the score is still tied after overtime, a **penalty shootout** is used to decide the winner. During these, each team gets three solo shots at the opponent's goal. If the game is still tied, the shootout continues until a team scores.

PRESEASON GAME

NHL AWARDS

HART MEMORIAL TROPHY

Given to the most valuable player (MVP) during the regular season

PENALTY SHOOTOUT

FROZEN PUCKS

Hockey pucks are made from hard rubber and can bounce wildly when hit hard. All NHL pucks are frozen for safety before and during games to reduce bouncing. They are replaced with a new frozen puck every 2 minutes during games.

ART ROSS TROPHY

Given to the player who has the most combined goals and assists at the end of the regular season

CONN SMYTHE TROPHY

Given to the MVP of the playoffs

PLAYOFF OVERTIME

During the playoffs, there are no shootouts. The longest NHL playoff game happened in 1936, when it took six overtime periods to decide the winner.

NHL teams' standings are determined by a point system during the regular season. A team receives two points for a win. They get one point if they lose in overtime or a shootout. A team receives no points if they lose in **regulation time**.

NHL PLAYOFFS

At the end of the season, the Stanley Cup **Playoffs** begin. The three teams in each division with the most points advance to the playoffs. Two **wild card** teams are also sent from each conference based on who has the highest point total. These 16 teams are arranged into a bracket based on conference and regular season point total. The teams with the highest amount of points play against the teams with the lowest amount of points. The team with the higher points in each matchup gets to play the first two games of the series in their home arenas. The teams then play two games in the lower ranked team's arena. If the series is still ongoing, the teams switch arenas until there is a winner.

The playoffs usually last around two months. Each playoff round is a best-of-seven series. The first team to win four games moves on to the next round. The final teams remaining from each conference face off to determine the Stanley Cup champion.

NHL HISTORY

Before 1917, professional hockey teams played in the National Hockey Association (NHA). This league ended because of disputes between team owners. Some former NHA owners began the NHL in Montréal, Canada, in 1917 with five Canadian teams. These teams were the Montréal Canadiens, Montréal Wanderers, Ottawa Senators, Quebec Bulldogs, and Toronto Arenas. The Bulldogs soon dropped out of the league. Their players joined the other four teams. The Arenas later became the Maple Leafs.

In 1924, the Boston Bruins joined the league as the first team from the United States. The league grew to 10 teams by 1926, six of which were from the U.S. But several of those early teams left the league. From 1942 to 1967, there were six NHL teams. These teams were the Boston Bruins, Chicago Blackhawks, Detroit Red Wings, Montréal Canadiens, New York Rangers, and Toronto Maple Leafs. These teams are now called the "Original Six."

The league grew and made changes in the 1930s and 1940s. The NHL held its first **All-Star Game** in 1947. In the 1949–50 season, the NHL schedule expanded to 70 games.

GAME TIME

NHL games are divided into three 20-minute periods. There is an 18-minute break between each period.

1929 BOSTON BRUINS

The league continued to grow and change in the 1960s. In 1963, the first NHL Draft was held. Six new U.S. teams joined the Original Six in 1967. In the 1968–69 season, the league expanded the schedule to 76 games. They expanded the schedule to 80 games for the 1974–75 season.

During the early 1970s, six more teams joined the NHL, bringing the total number of teams to 18. But in 1978, two of the teams merged, dropping the total number to 17. In 1979, the NHL merged with the World Hockey Association (WHA). Four WHA teams joined the NHL.

In just 12 years, the NHL had grown from six teams to 21 teams. Over the years, some of these teams relocated to new cities and took on new names. As the league expanded, teams were added in different cities. This meant that teams sometimes traveled long distances just to play another team in their own division. Before the 1981–82 season, the league realigned the conferences based on geography. Teams within the same divisions were now located closer together. Travel for games became easier.

HELMETS

In 1979, the league made a rule that all new players coming into the league had to wear helmets. In 1997, Craig MacTavish was the last NHL player to play without a helmet.

1997 JAPAN GAME

Between 1991 and 2000, the league expanded to include nine more teams. In 1997, two regular season NHL games were played in Japan. These were the first regular season NHL games played outside of North America. The NHL scheduled games in overseas locations many more times after that. They played regular season games in Sweden, Japan, Great Britain, Germany, Finland, and the Czech Republic. This gave fans in other countries a chance to cheer for their favorite teams and players in person.

2003 OUTDOOR GAME

In 2003, the NHL played its first regular season game outdoors in Edmonton, Canada. Because the outdoor game was so popular with fans, the NHL scheduled many more outdoor games in stadiums across North America. For many years, NHL games could end in a tie. But in 2005, the league added the shootout to games that remained tied in overtime. In 2017, the Vegas Golden Knights joined the league. The Seattle Kraken joined the league in 2021. This brought the total number of teams to 32.

TIMELINE

1917

The NHL is organized in Montréal, Canada

1924

The Boston Bruins become the first NHL team located in a U.S. city

1947

The NHL holds its first All-Star Game

1949

The NHL schedule expands to 70 games

1963

The NHL holds a draft for the first time

1974

The NHL schedule expands to 80 games

1979

The NHL merges with the WHA

1981

The NHL realigns conferences based on geography

2005

The NHL adds the shootout to decide tied games

2021

The NHL expands to 32 teams

1976–77 MONTRÉAL CANADIENS

The 1976–77 Montréal Canadiens team was loaded with talented players. They dominated games in the regular season and the playoffs. Head coach Scotty Bowman led the star-studded roster. Guy Lafleur, who played right wing, was a key part of this team. That season, he won the Art Ross Trophy after leading the league with 136 points. Left wing Steve Shutt led the league with 60 goals. Defensive players Larry Robinson, Serge Savard, and Guy Lapointe were called the "Big Three" because of their defensive skills. Robinson won the Norris Trophy that season. This award is given to the regular season's best defensive player in a year.

The Canadiens rolled through the regular season, winning a then-record 60 games. They won games by five goals or more 21 times. They are the only NHL team ever to play more than 60 games in a single season and lose fewer than 10. In the playoffs, they defeated the St. Louis Blues and the New York Islanders. They **swept** the Boston Bruins in the Stanley Cup Finals. It was their second championship in a row and the 20th in team history. The team's success extended over several seasons. The Canadiens won four straight Stanley Cups from 1976 to 1979.

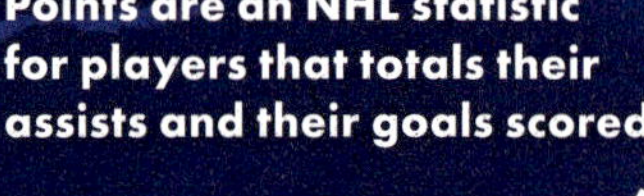

POINTS

Points are an NHL statistic for players that totals their assists and their goals scored.

SUPER STAR
GUY LAFLEUR
POSITION
RIGHT WING
KEY STAT
136 POINTS
GUY LAPOINTE
1976–77 RECORD
REGULAR SEASON
60—8—12
WIN LOSS TIE
QUARTERFINALS
4—0
SEMIFINALS
4—2
STANLEY CUP
4—0

1981–82 NEW YORK ISLANDERS

The New York Islanders were formed as an **expansion team** in 1972. But by the 1981–82 season, the Islanders were used to winning. They had already won the Stanley Cup in the previous two seasons.

The Islanders offense was anchored by the "Trio Grande" of future Hall of Famer forwards Mike Bossy, Bryan Trottier, and Clark Gillies. On defense, goalie Billy Smith won the season's Vezina Trophy. This trophy goes to the best goalie in a season. The Islanders won 54 games in the regular season, including a then-record 15 in a row.

The Islanders defeated the Pittsburgh Penguins and the New York Rangers in the first two rounds of the playoffs. The Islanders did not lose a game in the Conference Finals against the Quebec Nordiques. They swept the Vancouver Canucks to win the Stanley Cup Final. Bossy won the Conn Smythe Trophy after scoring 17 goals during the playoffs. The Islanders would win the Stanley Cup again in the 1982–83 season, becoming the first U.S. team to win four championships in a row.

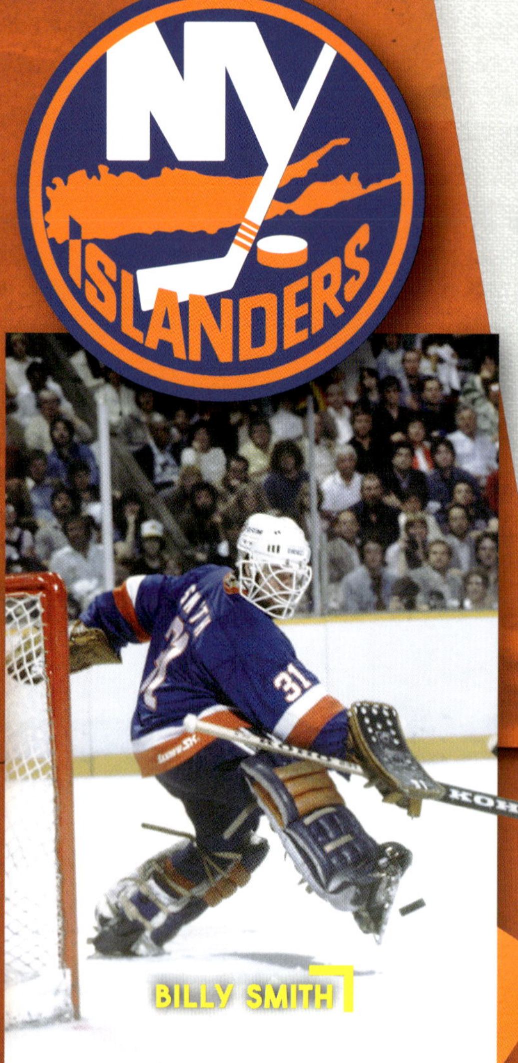

BILLY SMITH

VEZINA TROPHY

The Vezina Trophy is named after Georges Vézina. He played goalie for the Montréal Canadiens from 1917 to 1926.

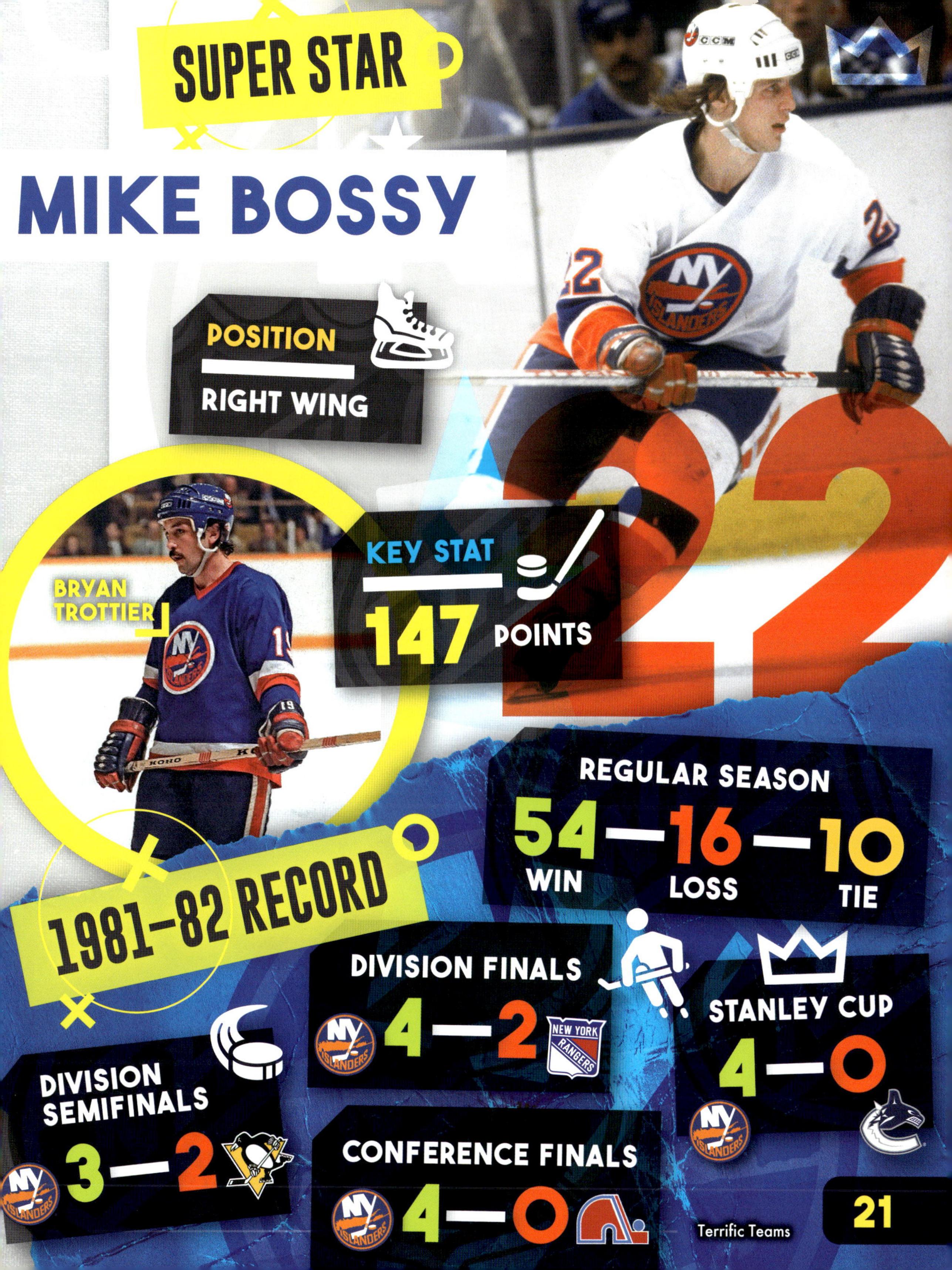
SUPER STAR
MIKE BOSSY
POSITION
RIGHT WING
BRYAN TROTTIER
KEY STAT
147 POINTS
1981–82 RECORD
REGULAR SEASON
54—16—10
WIN LOSS TIE
DIVISION SEMIFINALS
3—2
DIVISION FINALS
4—2
CONFERENCE FINALS
4—0
STANLEY CUP
4—0

1983–84 EDMONTON OILERS

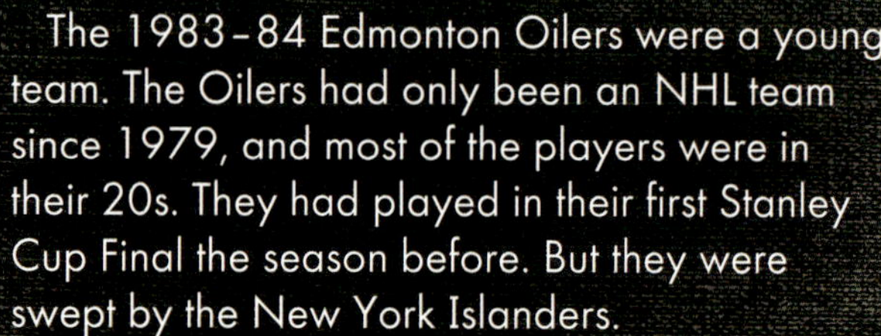

The 1983–84 Edmonton Oilers were a young team. The Oilers had only been an NHL team since 1979, and most of the players were in their 20s. They had played in their first Stanley Cup Final the season before. But they were swept by the New York Islanders.

Many of the Oilers' great players returned the next year. They were led by Wayne Gretzky, considered by many to be the greatest NHL player of all time. Other core players on the Oilers included Mark Messier, Jari Kurri, Glenn Anderson, Grant Fuhr, and Paul Coffey. The team was known for their speed and high-scoring offense. The team scored 446 goals that season for an average of 5.58 goals per game. These were both NHL records.

MARK MESSIER

In the 1984 Stanley Cup Final, the Oilers faced the Islanders in a rematch of the prior year. The Oilers won the series 4–1 and claimed the team's first ever Stanley Cup. The Oilers would go on to win the Stanley Cup four more times by 1990.

GRANT FUHR

1983–84 RECORD
REGULAR SEASON
57 — 18 — 5
WIN LOSS TIE
DIVISION SEMIFINALS
3 — 0
CONFERENCE FINALS
4 — 0
STANLEY CUP
4 — 1
DIVISION FINALS
4 — 3
SUPER STAR
WAYNE GRETZKY
POSITION
CENTER
KEY STAT
205 POINTS

2001-02 DETROIT RED WINGS

The 2001–02 Detroit Red Wings roster included 10 players that were Hall of Famers by the year 2024. The Red Wings' offense was powerful. Its stars included Brendan Shanahan, Sergei Fedorov, Brett Hull, Luc Robitaille, Steve Yzerman, and Igor Larionov. These players contributed 152 goals and 195 assists that season. They led a powerful offense that finished the regular season with 251 goals. Nicklas Lidström and Chris Chelios anchored the Red Wings defense. Dominik Hašek was the goalie. His strong play earned him the nickname "The Dominator." The Red Wings won 22 of their first 27 games. They finished the season with 51 wins.

The Red Wings got off to a wobbly start in the playoffs. They lost the first two playoff games to the Vancouver Canucks. Then they rallied to win four straight games, and their march through the playoffs began. The Red Wings defeated the Carolina Hurricanes in the Stanley Cup Finals. Lidström won the Conn Smythe Trophy after scoring 16 points in 23 games. He became the first European player in history to win the award.

NICKLAS LIDSTRÖM

SUPER STAR
BRENDAN SHANAHAN
POSITION
LEFT WING
KEY STAT
75 POINTS
DOMINIK HAŠEK
2001–02 RECORD
REGULAR SEASON
51—17—10—4
WIN LOSS TIE OVERTIME LOSS
CONFERENCE QUARTERFINALS
4—2
CONFERENCE SEMIFINALS
4—1
CONFERENCE FINALS
4—3
STANLEY CUP
4—1

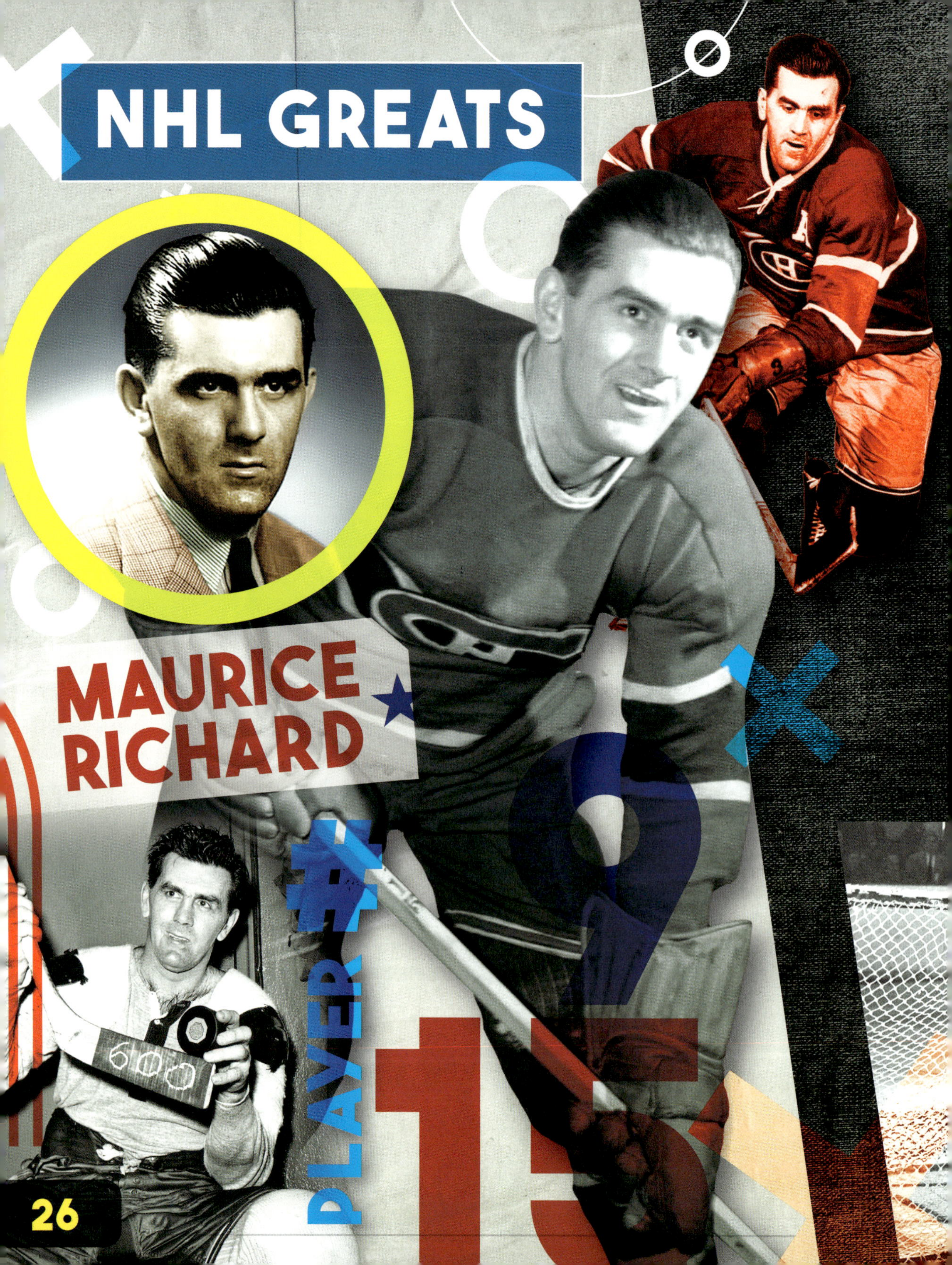
NHL GREATS
MAURICE
RICHARD
PLAYER #
9
15
600

Maurice Richard grew up in Montréal, Canada. He played hockey on school and neighborhood teams in the city. In 1942, he signed with the Montréal Canadiens. A teammate gave Richard the nickname "Rocket" because he moved so fast in practices.

In the 1944-45 season, Richard became the first player in NHL history to score 50 goals in 50 games. He won the Hart Memorial Trophy in the 1946-47 season as the league's MVP. Richard had a reputation for playing well under pressure. He scored 82 goals in 133 career playoff games, with 18 of them being the game-winning goal. Richard did not back down from fighting when games got rough. In 1955, he was suspended for the season after punching a referee in a fight. The next year Richard returned to playing, and the Canadiens won the first of five Stanley Cups in a row. In 1957, he became the first player in NHL history to score 500 career goals.

Richard played his whole career with the Canadiens. He won the Stanley Cup eight times in 18 seasons with the team. When he retired in 1960, Richard held several NHL records.

PROFILE

HEIGHT 5 FT 10 IN

BIRTHDAY AUGUST 4, 1921

POSITION RIGHT WING

YEAR SIGNED 1942

YEARS ACTIVE 1942–1960

TEAM

MONTRÉAL CANADIENS

MAURICE RICHARD TROPHY

Richard has a trophy named for him. The Maurice Richard Trophy is given to each regular season's goal-scoring leader.

AWARDS & RECORDS

978 GAMES PLAYED

422 ASSISTS

966 POINTS

544 GOALS

1961 ELECTED TO HOCKEY HALL OF FAME

1 HART MEMORIAL TROPHY

8 STANLEY CUP WINS

RICHARD'S 500TH GOAL

Gordie Howe started playing hockey at age 5. In 1946, he joined the Detroit Red Wings. Howe played for the Red Wings for 25 seasons. He helped the team win the Stanley Cup four times. Howe won six Art Ross Trophies and six Hart Memorial Trophies. He was known for his competitive spirit and his goal-scoring. He received the nickname "Mr. Hockey" because of his skill, toughness, and long-lasting impact on the sport.

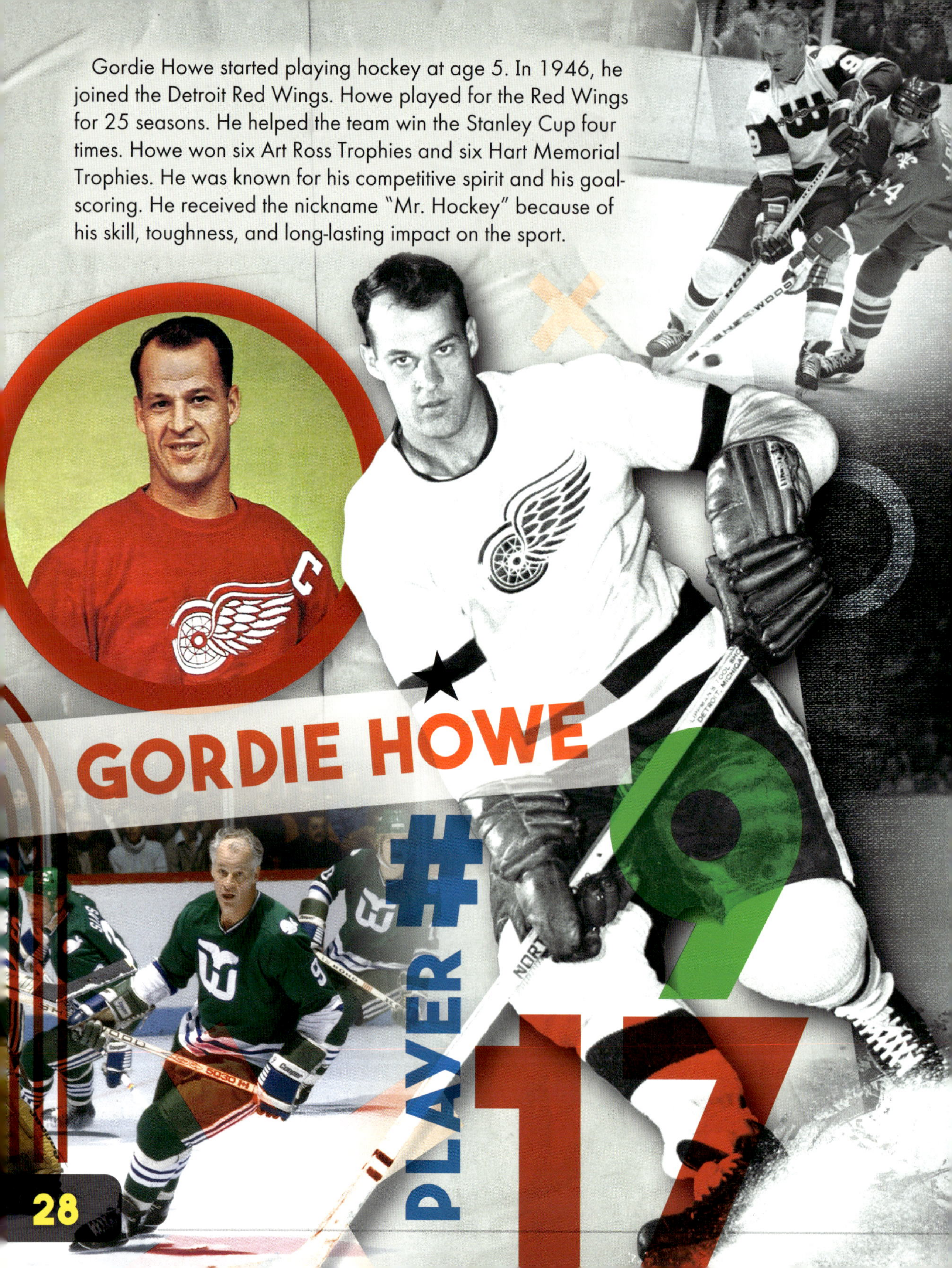

GORDIE HOWE

PLAYER #17

#9

Howe first retired in 1971. But his retirement did not last. In 1973, the 45-year-old Howe joined the Houston Aeros of the WHA to play with his sons Marty and Mark. He helped the team win the WHA championship in 1974 and 1975. He then joined the WHA's New England Whalers in 1977. In 1979, the Whalers joined the NHL as the Hartford Whalers. Howe continued to play for the team in the NHL. At 52 years old, he was the oldest person to ever play in the NHL. He played one season and retired again in 1980. In 2008, the NHL presented the first NHL Lifetime Achievement Award to Howe.

PROFILE

HEIGHT 6 FT 0 IN

BIRTHDAY MARCH 31, 1928

POSITION RIGHT WING

YEAR SIGNED 1946

YEARS ACTIVE 1946–1971, 1973–1980

TEAMS

DETROIT RED WINGS

HARTFORD WHALERS

AWARDS & RECORDS

1,049 ASSISTS

1,767 GAMES PLAYED

1,850 POINTS

801 GOALS

1972 ELECTED TO HOCKEY HALL OF FAME

6 ART ROSS TROPHIES

6 HART MEMORIAL TROPHIES

2008 NHL LIFETIME ACHIEVEMENT AWARD

4 STANLEY CUP WINS

BOBBY ORR

Bobby Orr began skating when he was 4 years old. He started playing in hockey leagues when he was in kindergarten. Orr was first noticed by scouts from the Boston Bruins at age 12. The team signed him to an **amateur** contract two years later. Four years later, in 1966, he played his first games with the Bruins.

Orr's speed and shot-blocking skills on defense earned him the Norris Trophy in eight straight seasons. He won the Conn Smythe Trophy twice after leading the Bruins to Stanley Cup victories in 1970 and 1972. Orr played 10 seasons for the Bruins before signing with the Chicago Blackhawks after the 1976 season. Orr struggled with knee injuries and retired in 1978 at age 30. He was inducted into the Hockey Hall of Fame in 1979.

Despite his shortened career, Orr changed hockey because he was a defenseman who also scored many goals. Before Orr played, defensive players protected their own goal and offensive players scored. Orr remains the only defenseman to lead the NHL in scoring, an achievement he accomplished twice. He still holds the NHL record for most points scored by a defenseman in a single season.

WAYNE GRETZKY
PLAYER #99
RANGERS
OILERS
C
TPM2020
Supra

Many sportswriters and hockey fans agree that Wayne Gretzky is the greatest hockey player of all time. His play earned him the nickname "The Great One." Gretzky was 2 years old when he first skated and began to learn hockey. He signed with the WHA's Indianapolis Racers in 1978. They soon traded him to the Edmonton Oilers, who joined the NHL in 1979.

Gretzky played for the Oilers for nine seasons, leading them to four Stanley Cup victories. He led the league in scoring for nine straight seasons. In the 1981–82 season, he scored 92 goals and set the NHL single-season goals record. In 1988, Gretzky was traded to the Los Angeles Kings. He helped increase hockey's popularity in the U.S. He later played for the St. Louis Blues and New York Rangers before retiring in 1999. At the time of his retirement, Gretzky held over 60 NHL records. His nine Hart Memorial Trophies are the most won by any player in NHL history. He also remains the NHL's all-time points leader. After Gretzky retired, the NHL retired his number. No other NHL player will ever wear a number 99 jersey.

PROFILE

HEIGHT 6 FT 0 IN

BIRTHDAY JANUARY 26, 1961

POSITION CENTER

YEAR SIGNED 1978

YEARS ACTIVE 1978–1999

TEAMS

EDMONTON OILERS

LOS ANGELES KINGS

ST. LOUIS BLUES

NEW YORK RANGERS

AWARDS & RECORDS

1,487 GAMES PLAYED

1,963 ASSISTS

2,857 POINTS

894 GOALS

1999 ELECTED TO HOCKEY HALL OF FAME

10 ART ROSS TROPHIES

9 HART MEMORIAL TROPHIES

4 STANLEY CUP WINS

HAT TRICKS

Wayne Gretzky holds the NHL record for most hat tricks with 50.

JAROMÍR JÁGR

Jaromír Jágr was born in Czechoslovakia and played professional hockey there as a teenager. In 1990, he became the first Czechoslovakian to enter the NHL Draft. The Pittsburgh Penguins drafted him, and he scored 27 goals in his first season. The Penguins won the Stanley Cup that year and the next. By the end of his career, Jágr had played for nine different NHL teams. He also played professional hockey in Russia and the Czech Republic.

Jágr won the Art Ross Trophy in five seasons. He won the Hart Memorial Trophy in 1999. He finished his career with 1,921 total points, the second most of all time. Jágr had 766 goals and 1,155 assists during his career. He is one of the most productive European players to play in the NHL. Jágr also won an Olympic gold medal with the Czech Republic at the 1998 Winter Olympics. He is a member of the Triple Gold Club. This describes players who have won the Stanley Cup, the International Ice Hockey World Championship, and an Olympic gold medal.

BIRTHDAY FEBRUARY 15, 1972

POSITION RIGHT WING

YEAR SIGNED 1990

YEARS ACTIVE 1990–2018

PITTSBURGH PENGUINS

WASHINGTON CAPITALS

NEW YORK RANGERS

PHILADELPHIA FLYERS

DALLAS STARS

BOSTON BRUINS

NEW JERSEY DEVILS

FLORIDA PANTHERS

CALGARY FLAMES

1,733 GAMES PLAYED

1,155 ASSISTS

1,921 POINTS

766 GOALS

5 ART ROSS TROPHIES

1 HART MEMORIAL TROPHY

2 STANLEY CUP WINS

ALEX OVECHKIN
PLAYER #8

Alex Ovechkin played hockey for a Russian professional team when he was just 16. The Washington Capitals drafted Ovechkin in 2004. In his first year, he won the Calder Memorial Trophy. This award goes to the best **rookie** in a season. Ovechkin played in his first NHL All-Star Game in the 2006–07 season.

The Capitals finished last in their division in Ovechkin's first two seasons. But in the 2007–08 season, Ovechkin scored 65 goals and helped the Capitals win the division title. Ovechkin led the league in scoring for four straight seasons from 2013 to 2016. In 2017–18, Ovechkin led the league with 49 goals. The Capitals won the Stanley Cup. Ovechkin was the first Russian player to captain a Stanley Cup winning team. He won the Conn Smythe Trophy that year. Ovechkin has scored 50 or more goals in nine different seasons. Only two other NHL players have achieved nine 50-goal seasons. Ovechkin won the Maurice Richard Trophy in nine seasons as the league's leading scorer. He won the Hart Memorial Trophy three times. In 2025, he broke Wayne Gretzky's career goals record. He remains the NHL's all-time leading goal scorer.

MEMORABLE MOMENTS

CANADIENS' FIVE STRAIGHT STANLEY CUPS

Winning the Stanley Cup is a huge achievement for any NHL team. But on April 14, 1960, the Montréal Canadiens did something no other NHL team has done. On that date, the Canadiens won the Stanley Cup for the fifth year in a row.

The Canadiens' strong offense was led by Jean Béliveau, Henri Richard, and Bernie Geoffrion. Their defense was anchored by Norris Trophy winners Doug Harvey and Tom Johnson. Goalie Jacques Plante won the Vezina Trophy as the NHL's best goaltender in all five seasons that the Canadiens won the Stanley Cup.

The Canadiens swept the Chicago Blackhawks in the playoffs to reach the Stanley Cup Final. The championship series matched up the Canadiens against the Toronto Maple Leafs. The Canadiens won Game 1 by a score of 4–2. They secured a narrow victory in Game 2, winning 2–1. Game 3 saw the Canadiens win 5–2. On April 14, they won Game 4 by a score of 4–0 to sweep the series. No other NHL team has won more than four Stanley Cups in a row. By winning five, the Canadiens put themselves into NHL history as one of the greatest **dynasties** of all time.

JACQUES PLANTE

JEAN BÉLIVEAU

LEAGUE LEADERS

The Montréal Canadiens have won the Stanley Cup 24 times. This is the most of any NHL team.

GRETZKY'S 802ND GOAL

On March 23, 1994, Wayne Gretzky scored his 802nd regular-season goal and earned a place in the record books as the NHL's all-time leader in goals. Before that game, the record of 801 goals belonged to Gordie Howe. Growing up, Gretzky had admired Howe as a hockey hero.

Gretzky's record-setting goal happened in a game between the Los Angeles Kings and the Vancouver Canucks. The Kings had a one-man advantage after a Canucks player was sent to the penalty box. Luc Robitaille handled the puck and passed it to Gretzky, who passed it to Marty McSorley. Canucks goalie Kirk McLean closed in on McSorley. But McSorley passed back to Gretzky. With a wide-open net, Gretzky scored! He had broken what many thought was an unbreakable record. Gretzky would go on to score 894 goals before he retired in 1999. His record stood for more than 30 years before being broken by Alex Ovechkin in 2025.

BERGERON'S GAME WINNER

PATRICE BERGERON

In 2013, the Boston Bruins faced the Toronto Maple Leafs in Game 7 of the Eastern Conference Quarterfinals. The Maple Leafs held on to a 4-1 lead midway through the third period. Bruins right wing Nathan Horton found the net to bring the Bruins within two goals with just over 10 minutes left to play. But the Bruins struggled to score another goal.

Time started to run out. The Bruins pulled their goalie in favor of another player on the ice. With 1:22 left in the game, Bruins left wing Milan Lucic scored to make it a one-goal game. Seconds later, Bruins center Patrice Bergeron took a long shot over the shoulder of Maple Leafs goalie James Reimer to tie the game.

The game went into overtime. With 13:55 left, the Bruins got a shot on the goal. Reimer saved it. But the puck was hit away from him. Bergeron got the puck and fired a shot. Score! The Bruins won the game and the series.

BERGERON'S GAME-WINNING GOAL

BRUINS CELEBRATE OVERTIME VICTORY

THE NHL BY THE NUMBERS

THE NHL WAS FOUNDED IN **1917**. THE FIRST NHL GAME WAS PLAYED ON **DECEMBER 19, 1917**.

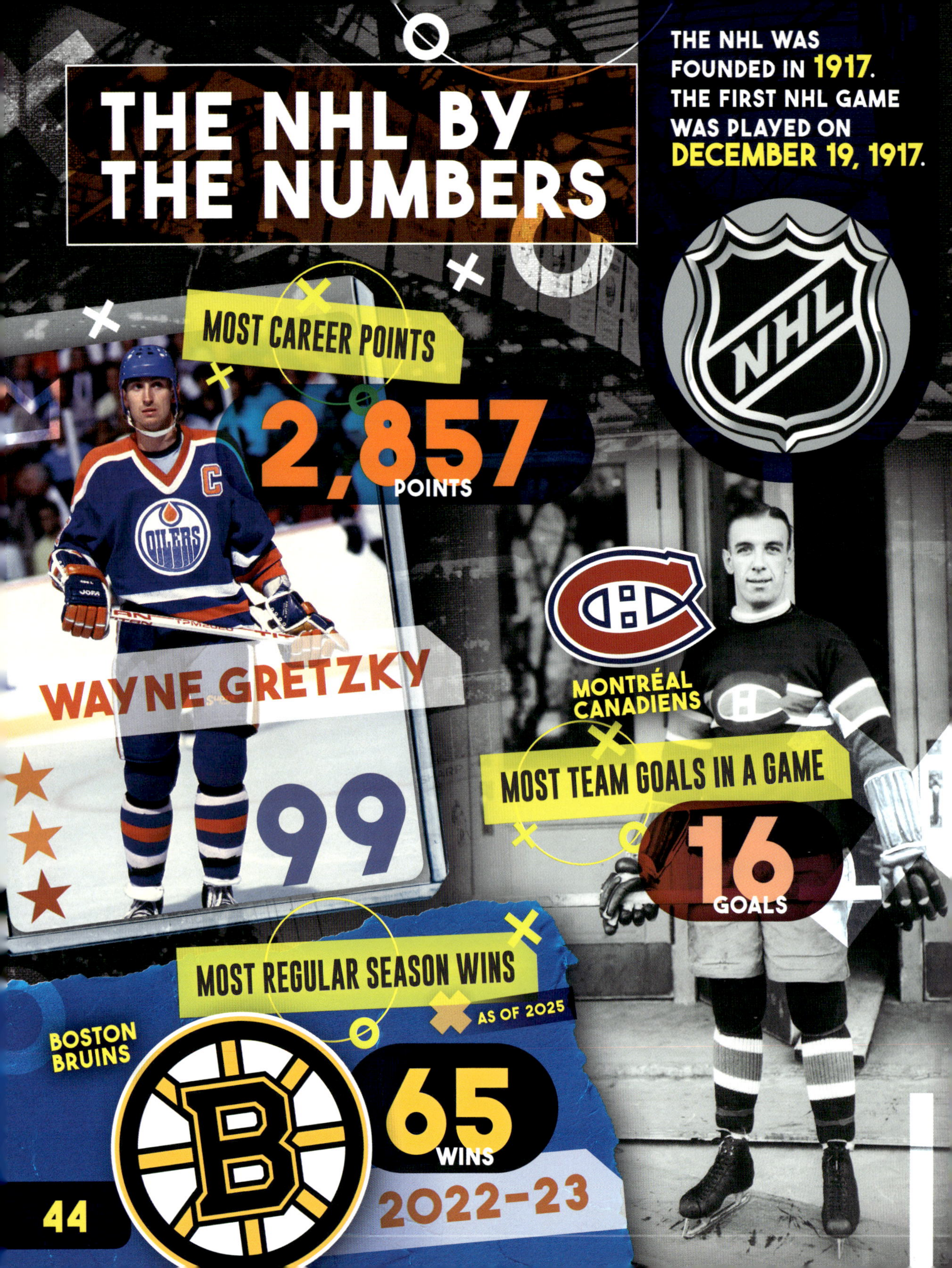

OLDEST TEAM
FOUNDED 1909
JOINED THE NHL IN 1917
MONTRÉAL CANADIENS
12
MOST CAREER GOALS
AS OF 2025
ALEX OVECHKIN
897
GOALS
MOST GAMES PLAYED
1,779
GAMES
PATRICK MARLEAU
LARGEST STADIUM
BELL CENTRE, MONTREAL, CANADA
21,273
PEOPLE
MOST STANLEY CUPS
AS OF 2025
MONTRÉAL CANADIENS
24
CUPS
MOST CAREER ASSISTS
WAYNE GRETZKY
1,963
ASSISTS

GLOSSARY

affiliate—related to a team connected to a major league team

All-Star Game—a game between the best players in a league

amateur—related to people who are not paid for an activity

conference—a grouping of teams that often compete against each other

division—a group of teams that often play each other

draft—a process during which professional teams choose high school and college athletes to play for them

dynasties—teams that dominate their sport or league for an extended amount of time

expansion team—a new team added to a sports league

hat trick—an event where a player scores three or more goals in one game

minor league—related to a professional hockey league that is below the National Hockey League

offseason—the time in between seasons of a sports league

penalty shootout—a way to end overtime games where single players from each team try to score goals against the opposing team's goalie until one side scores more than the other

playoffs—games played after the regular season is over; playoff games determine which teams play in the championship.

preseason—games played before the regular season; preseason games do not count towards a team's record.

regulation time—the typical length of a game without any overtime added

rookie—a first-year player in a sports league

swept—won a series of games without any losses

wild card—related to teams that reach the postseason even though they do not win their division

WRITE ABOUT IT!

- Many people think Wayne Gretzky is the greatest player in NHL history. Do you agree with them? If yes, why do you think he is the greatest? If no, who do you think is the greatest and **why?**

- The NHL has undergone many changes in its history. Which one do **you** think was the most important?

- **What** do you think was the greatest moment in NHL history?

INDEX

The images in this book are reproduced through the courtesy of: All-Pro Reels/ Wikimedia Commons, front cover, pp. 1, 36 (all), 45 (Ovechkin), 46 (main); Governor Tom Wolf/ Wikimedia Commons, front cover, p. 1; Alex Goykhman/ Wikimedia Commons, front cover, p. 1; Francis Specker/ Alamy Stock Photo, front cover, p. 1; Marty Ellis, front cover, p. 1; Tony Triolo/ Getty Images, pp. 2, 14 (bottom), 19, 30; Bibliothèque et Archives nationales du Québec/ Wikimedia Commons, pp. 2, 26; B Bennett/ Getty Images, pp. 3, 17 (1974, 1979), 21, 23, 32 (main, inset, top), 33, 39 (all), 40 (inset), 45 (Gretzky); National Hockey League/ Getty Images, pp. 4, 7, 8 (left), 9 (main, Conn trophy), 12 (fun fact), 14 (top); Associated Press/ AP Images, pp. 5 (all), 6 (all), 8 (Hart trophy inset), 16, 18, 20 (left), 24 (left), 26 (bottom, top), 28 (main, top), 30 (inset), 34 (bottom), 38; Getty Images Sport/ Getty Images, p. 8 (top); Bruce Bennett/ Getty Images, pp. 8 (Hart trophy), 22 (left), 44 (Gretzky); Kevin Brine, p. 9 (fun fact); Brian Babineau/ Getty Images, pp. 9 (Art trophy), 43; Steve/ Wikimedia Commons, p. 9 (Art trophy inset); Andy/ Wikimedia Commons, p. 9 (Conn trophy inset); Josh Lavallee/ Getty Images, p. 10; Jonathan Kozub/ Getty Images, p. 10 (inset); Klara_Steffkova, pp. 11, 45; FPG/ Getty Images, p. 12; Archives of Ontario/ Wikimedia Commons, p. 13; Bettmann/ Getty Images, pp. 13 (bottom), 29, 30 (top, bottom), 31, 44 (Canadians); Denis Brodeur/ Getty Images, pp. 14 (middle), 15, 28 (bottom); Graig Abel/ Getty Images, pp. 15 (fun fact), 21 (inset); Dave Sandford/ Getty Images, pp. 16 (inset), 25; Felix Mizioznikov, p. 17 (1924); Doug Benc/ Getty Images, p. 17 (2005); George Gojkovich/ Getty Images, p. 19 (inset); Peter Read Miller/ Getty Images, p. 20 (right); Focus On Sport/ Getty Images, pp. 22 (right), 34 (main), 48 (main); Sporting News Archive/ Getty Images, p. 24 (right); Tom Pidgeon/ Getty Images, p. 25 (inset); JonnyThunnder/ Wikimedia Commons, p. 26 (inset); National Film Board of Canada/ Wikimedia Commons, p. 27; Kmf164/ Wikimedia Commons, p. 27 (fun fact); Ralston-Purina Company/ Wikimedia Commons, p. 28 (inset); Hakandahlstrom/ Wikimedia Commons, p. 32 (left); Eliot J. Schechter/ Getty Images, p. 34 (inset); Jim McIsaac/ Getty Images, p. 34 (top); Jamie Sabau/ Getty Images, p. 35; AlexanderJonesi/ Wikimedia Commons, p. 37; Robert Beck/ Getty Images, pp. 40, 41 (all); Jared Wickerham/ Getty Images, p. 42 (top, middle); Steve Babineau/ Getty Images, p. 42 (bottom); TimelessPerspectives, p. 45 (stadium); Brandon Magnus/ Getty Images, p. 45 (Marleau); David S Baum, pp. 44-45 (background).